Investigate the natural and human features of Australia as you practise your NSW Foundation style handwriting.

My name is

My school is

My favourite place in Australia is

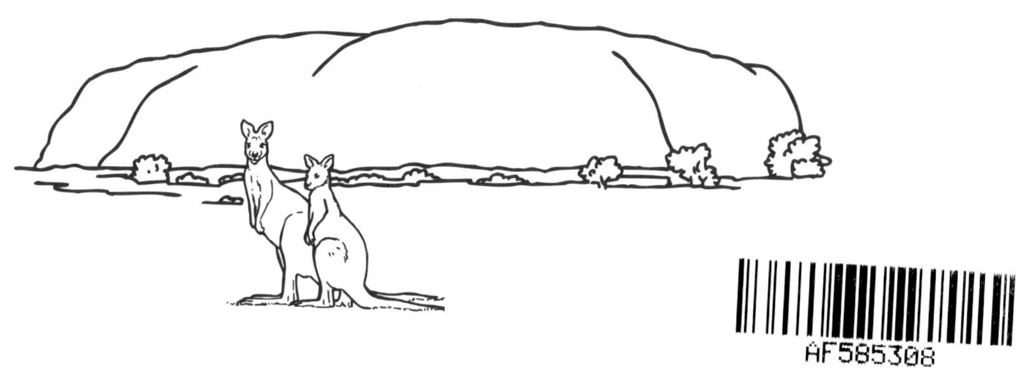

AF585308

**Learning goal:** To improve knowledge of the alphabet in NSW Foundation style handwriting

**Success criteria:**

- I can trace and write all lower-case and capital letters of the alphabet in NSW Foundation style using both printing and cursive.
- I can trace and write all lower-case and capital letters of the alphabet in NSW Foundation style using appropriate size, spacing and slope.

# Are you ready to write?

## Posture

Ensure your feet are flat on the floor and you are sitting well back in the chair.

## Paper position

left-handed

Hold the paper with your non-writing hand.

right-handed

## Pencil grip

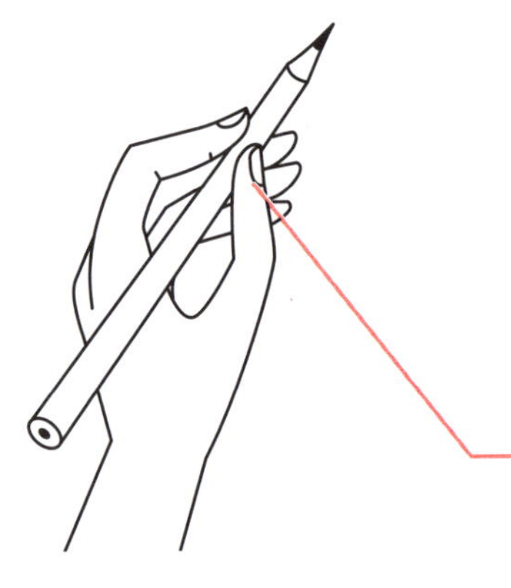

left-handed

Hold your pencil with one finger on top of the barrel.

Support the barrel with your thumb.

right-handed

# Foundation printing

Copy the Foundation alphabet. Circle the letters that spell the word 'geography'.

Copy the letters with an anti-clockwise movement.

Copy the letters with a clockwise movement.

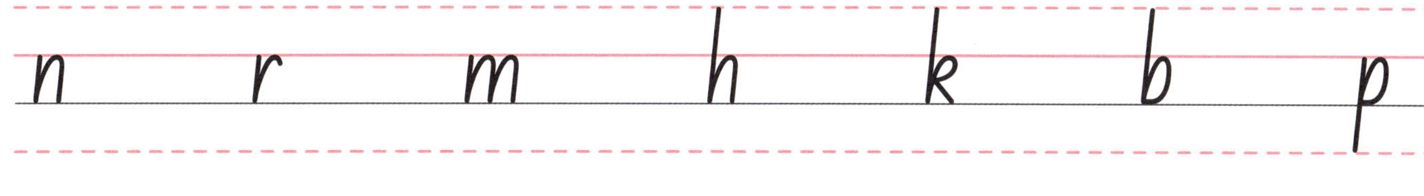


Copy the letters with a downstroke movement.

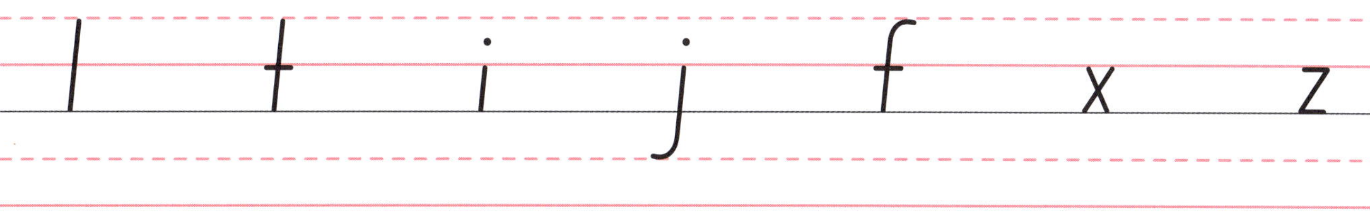


ISBN: 9780170416924

Trace the capital letters.

A B C D E F G H I J K

L M N O P Q R S T U V W

X Y Z

Copy the definitions for 'habitat' and 'ecosystem'.

HABITAT: a specific place where a plant or animal lives.

ECOSYSTEM: all the living things that interact in the environment of an area.

# Self-assessment: Foundation printing

Copy the place names in printing, then in capital letters.

New South Wales

NEW SOUTH WALES NSW

Wollongong WOLLONGONG

Dubbo DUBBO

Gundagai GUNDAGAI

## Self-assessment

Rate your printing and capital letters.

☐ I need more practice.

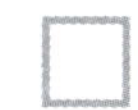

They are improving.

They look great!

ISBN: 9780170416924

# Exits and entries

These are the exit letters. Remember: an exit flick is a way out of a letter. It helps you join to the next letter.

a d h i k l m n t u v w x

Trace and copy the exit letters.

a d h i k l m

n t u v w x

These are the entry letters. Remember: an entry is a way into a letter. It helps you join to the letter.

i j m n p r u v w y

Trace and copy the entry letters.

i j m n p r u v w y

Copy the alphabet. Then circle each letter that has both an exit and an entry.

m → m

a b c d e f g h i j k l m

n o p q r s t u v w x y z

Practise your exits and entries. Trace and copy these geographical concepts.

place space sustainability

environment interconnection

Write a sentence using one or more of the words above. Circle each letter with both an entry and an exit.

ISBN: 9780170416924

# Self-assessment: Exits and entries

Trace around the maps of Australia and write the exit and entry letters under the correct headings.

Exit-only letters (7)

Entry only letters (4)

Letters with exits and entries (6)

get.ga/PMWA90

## Self-assessment

How well do you know your exit and entry letters?

| | | |
|---|---|---|
| ☐ I need to more practice. | ☐ I know most of them. | ☐ I know them well! |

## Diagonal joins

Extend the exit flick of the first letter to join to the second letter.

Trace the first letter and join to the second letter using a straight, quick diagonal line.

am ci eu nn hi

Trace and copy these letter pairs with diagonal joins.

ap dj ev aw ty di au av

Trace and copy these words with diagonal joins.

Uluru live never upper distance

happen evening away because

didgeridoo diagram hide city

# Diagonal joins to head and body letters

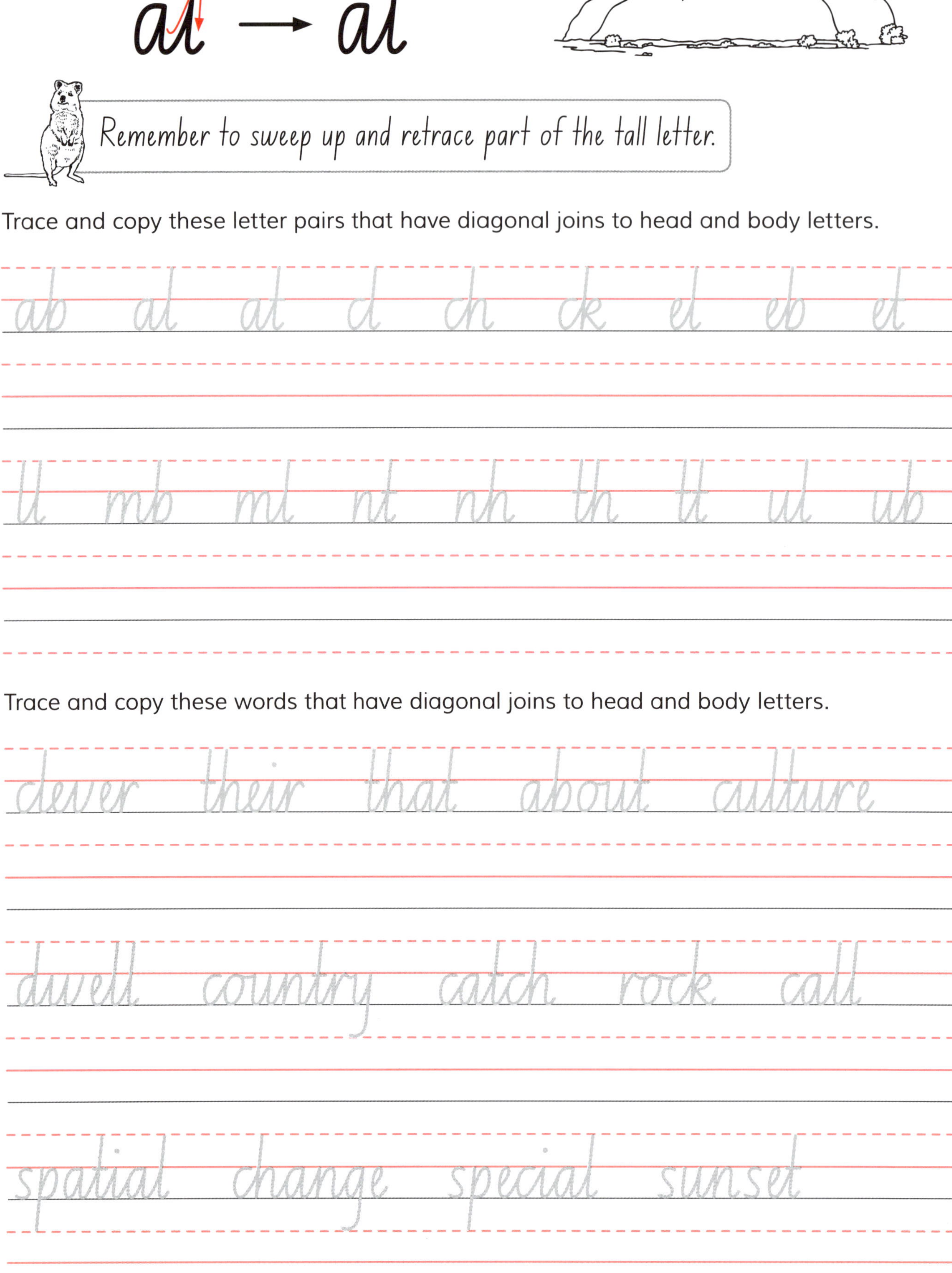


*Remember to sweep up and retrace part of the tall letter.*

Trace and copy these letter pairs that have diagonal joins to head and body letters.

Trace and copy these words that have diagonal joins to head and body letters.

# Diagonal joins from 'q'

A 'q' can be tricky: you need to quickly change direction and go all the way to the top of the next letter.

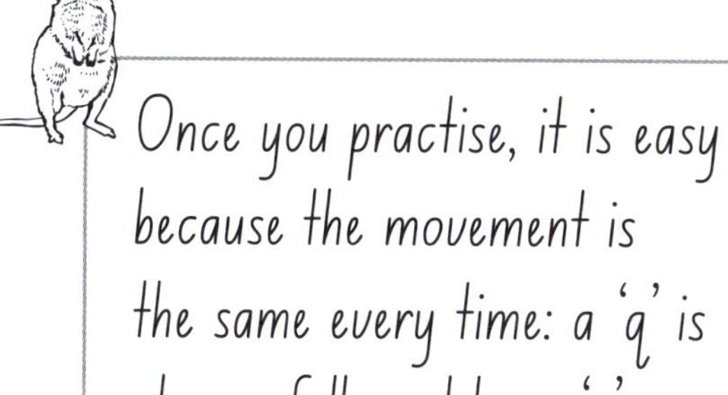

Once you practise, it is easy because the movement is the same every time: a 'q' is always followed by a 'u'.

Trace and copy.

qu qu qu qu qu qu qu qu

question quoll quokka equal

Trace and copy.

Clever geography students ask

questions about the natural habitat

of quolls and quokkas.

ISBN: 9780170416924

# Diagonal joins from 'z'

Remember to make a little wave with your pencil before joining 'z' to the next letter.

Trace and copy.

zi zl zy ze zu

zip zero lazy wheeze zebra

Trace and copy.

A camel ride is an amazing way to experience Uluru. After a lazy snooze, wake up ready to see the rock ablaze with sunset colours.

ISBN: 9780170416924

## Self-assessment: Diagonal joins

Copy the text. Remember to be careful with your diagonal joins.

The traditional custodians of the

Uluru area are the Anangu

Aboriginal people. The Anangu people

have decided visitors may not climb

the rock as it is a sacred place.

### Self-assessment

Rate your diagonal joins.

☐ I need practice.

☐ They are improving.

☐ They are great!

ISBN: 9780170416924

## Drop-in joins

a c d g o q

Great Barrier Reef

Remember: when joining diagonally to one of these letters, make a long exit, then lift your pencil and drop in the second letter.

long exit and pencil lift

ma

Trace.

a c d g o q

Trace and copy these letter pairs with drop-in joins.

ac co id ug no ic ua ud

ag aq ma uc ad ig eq cc

Copy these words. Change colour when you do a drop-in join.

great sea marine algae

ISBN: 9780170416924

Copy these words with drop-in joins. The red dots show which joins are drop-in joins.

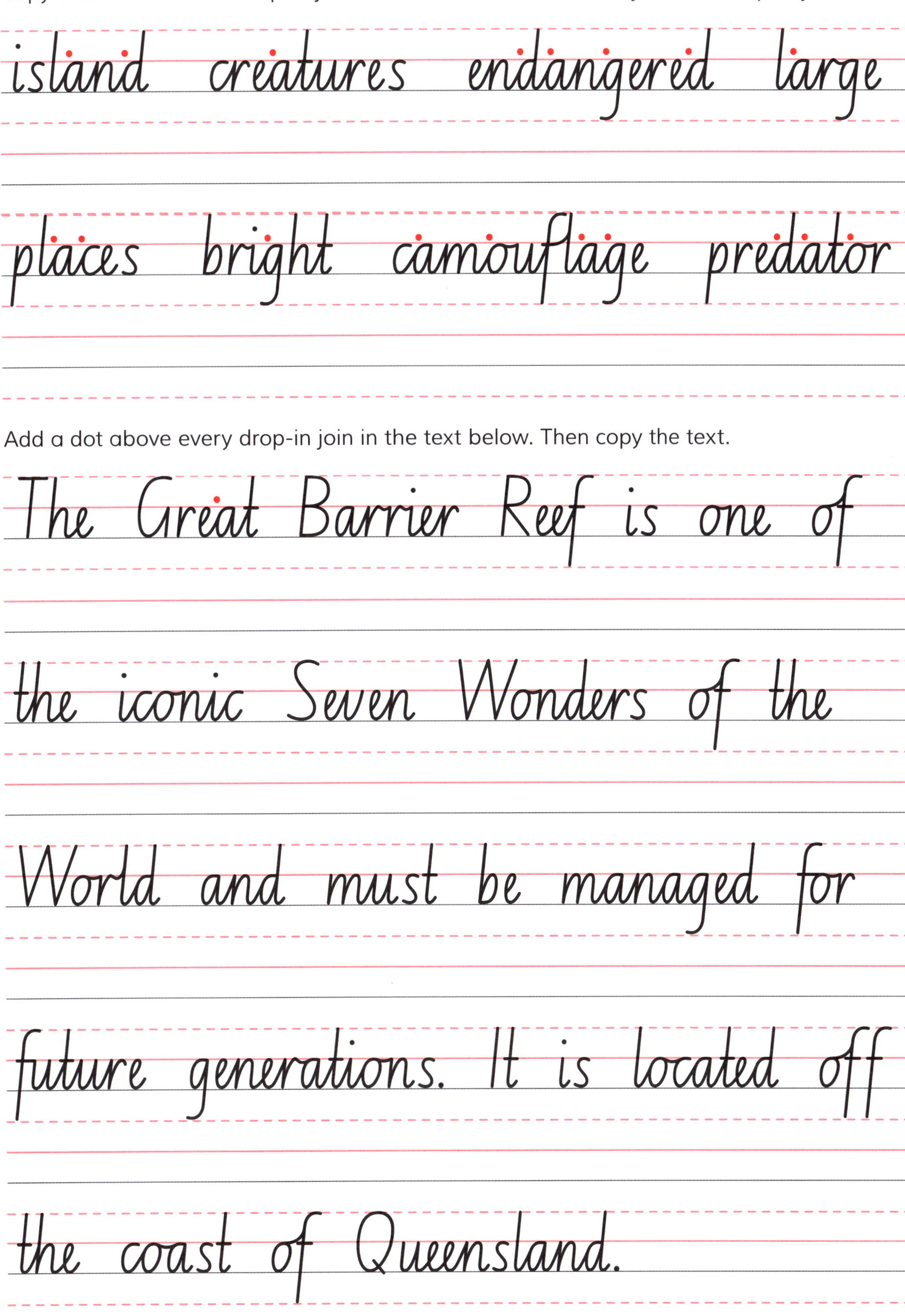


Add a dot above every drop-in join in the text below. Then copy the text.



ISBN: 9780170416924

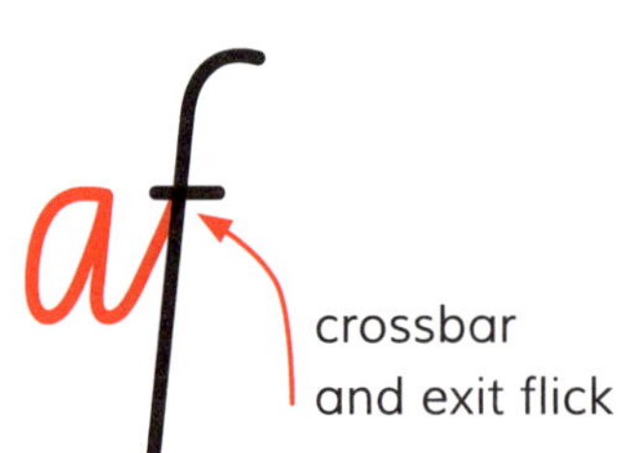


Remember: when dropping in 'f', extend the exit flick of the letter before it, then make sure the crossbar meets the exit flick.

Trace these letter pairs with 'f' dropped in.

af ef if uf nf lf mf

Trace and copy.

lift reef effect harmful

shelf difference lifesaving

Trace and copy this joke.

Q: What does the cuttlefish say to the reef when the tide comes in?

A: Long time, no sea.

ISBN: 9780170416924

## Self-assessment: Drop-in joins

Copy the text. Remember to be careful with your drop-in joins.

People who live in Australia love to spend time by the water. Fun aquatic sports include surfing and canoeing. After these activities, it is refreshing to eat an ice block.

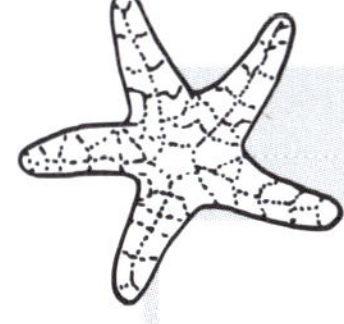

### Self-assessment

Rate your drop-in joins.

|  |  |  |
|---|---|---|
| ☐ | ☐ | ☐ |
| I need practice. | I am getting better. | My use of drop-in joins is excellent! |

ISBN: 9780170416924

# Horizontal joins

o r v w x

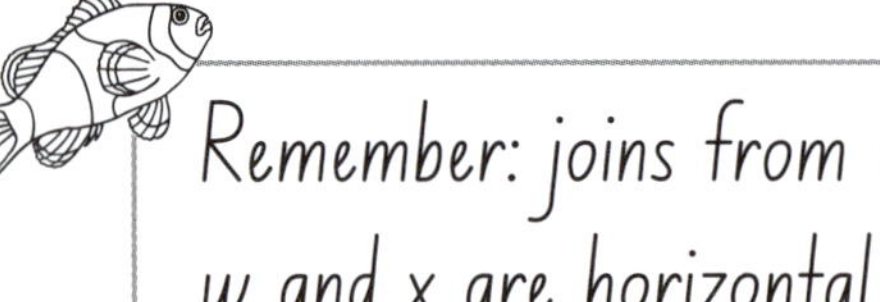


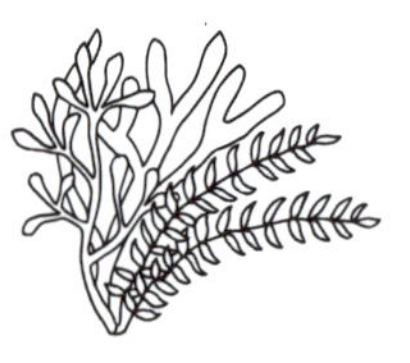

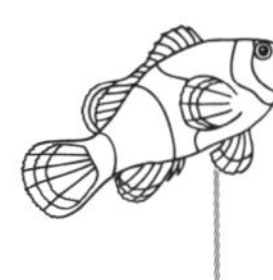

Remember: 'x' can be joined or unjoined to the next letter.

Trace and copy these letter pairs with horizontal joins.

or rm wr ox rr xi xy xy wn om

wm on rn op ri vy wi ov ru vi

wy ow oy vu wp oj oi ou rp

Trace and copy these words with horizontal joins.

enjoy exit bright without

swim country town anxious

# Horizontal joins to anti-clockwise letters

Remember: when making a horizontal join to an anti-clockwise letter, a little retracing is required.

Trace and copy these letter pairs and words with horizontal joins to anti-clockwise letters.

ro ra wa va ro ra wa va

rainfall vary water coral protect

od oc vo oa rd od oc vo oa rd

codfish ocean evolve road border

ISBN: 9780170416924

# Horizontal joins to head and body letters

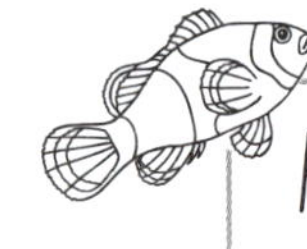

Remember to sweep up and retrace a little.

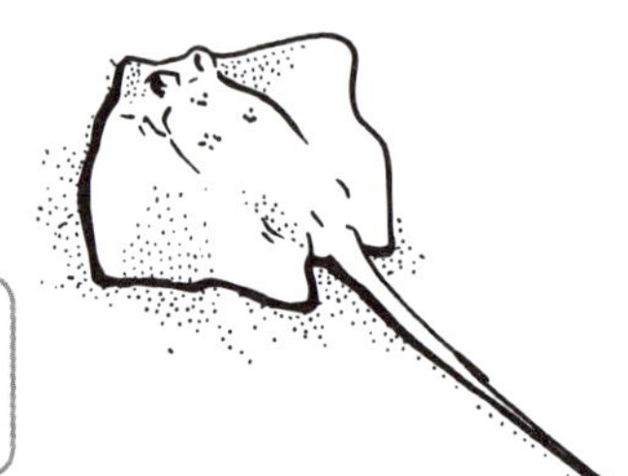

Make your own letter pairs that have horizontal joins to head and body letters.

o r v w x to b h k l t

ob

Trace and copy these words. Underline each horizontal join to a head and body letter.

world polyps white throttle pearl

colours bottle hollow whales next

Trace and copy these horizontal join patterns.

rlrl ohoh olol whwh

ISBN: 9780170416924

# Horizontal joins from 'f'

fu fi fa fo

When joining to letters from 'f', use a straight horizontal line to the next letter. Retrace when joining from 'f' to 'a' or 'o'.

Trace and copy.

fin fish force follow waterfall

fun family playful fantastic fit

fl

Remember: when 'f' joins to 'l', retrace the downstroke of the 'l'.

Trace and copy.

flight flounder fly flap flow

fe

Remember: 'f' doesn't join to 'e'.

Trace and copy.

fern feral fear few fell feet

ISBN: 9780170416924

## Self-assessment: Horizontal joins

Copy the text. Remember to be careful with your horizontal joins.

Swimming and snorkelling in the
Great Barrier Reef can be so much
fun. You may see colourful fish and
coral, or even a whale. We must
try to protect this unique ecosystem.

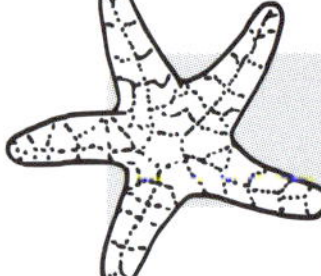

### Self-assessment

Rate your horizontal joins.

☐ I need practice.

☐ They are getting better.

☐ My horizontal joins are excellent!

ISBN: 9780170416924

# Letters that do not join

Remember: letters that finish in a clockwise direction do not join to the next letter.

Find, trace and copy only the six letters below that do not join to the next letter.

b c d z y i g s j u p

Put a red dot where there will be no join in cursive.

| | | | |
|---|---|---|---|
| sun | erosion | geography | project |
| helicopter | visit | ships | Apostles |
| flight | limestone | stacks | coastline |

Prove your answers by writing the words in cursive.

ISBN: 9780170416924

Write the plural forms of the words below by adding 's'. Circle the clockwise finishing letters in each word. Did you remember to leave them unjoined?

stack layer stone sunset light

boardwalk plant seagull bridge

island journey ship measurement

Copy the text and circle the non-joining letter pairs.

The sight of the Twelve Apostles is

breathtaking. Flying over the sea in

a helicopter gives a wonderful view.

get.ga/PMWA93

ISBN: 9780170416924

## Self-assessment: Letters that do not join

Rewrite the text below in cursive. Remember to take care with letters that do not join.

The Twelve Apostles are located in the Port Campbell National Park along the Great Ocean Road in Victoria. The unique limestone stacks were created by the erosion of the mainland cliffs.

### Self-assessment

Rate your knowledge of the letters that do not join.

☐ I'm just getting started.

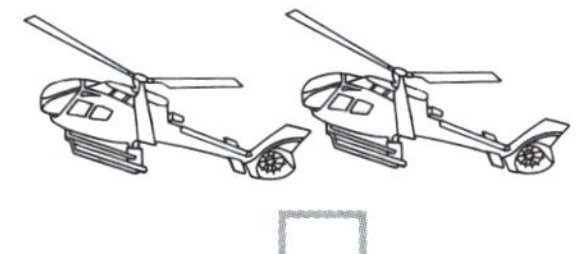

☐ I'm taking off.

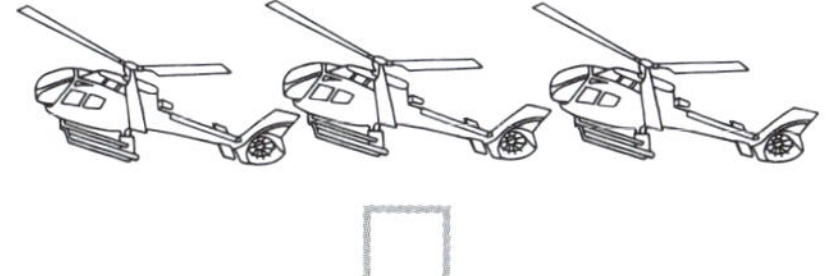

☐ I'm flying high!

ISBN: 9780170416924

## Size: Using smaller writing lines

Smaller writing lines help you to write more quickly. Try to keep your letters a consistent size. It will make your writing easier to read.

Practise using smaller writing lines. Copy the text.

The amazing Naracoorte Caves are located in South Australia. They are part of a World Heritage site. There are many large caves at Naracoorte that have acted as animal traps for over 500 000 years. The fossils inside are of great interest to palaeontologists.

## Self-assessment: Using smaller writing lines

From the clues below, use Foundation printing to write the names of Kangaroo Island, Naracoorte Caves and Adelaide in their correct locations on the map.

- People can take a ferry to Kangaroo Island.
- Naracoorte Caves are located near the border between South Australia and Victoria.
- Adelaide is located north-east of Kangaroo Island.

### Self-assessment

Rate how easy to read your handwriting is in smaller lines.

  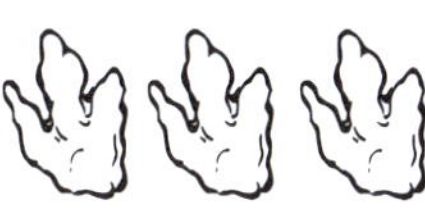

| ☐ I can improve. | ☐ I'm getting there. | ☐ I'm doing well! |
|---|---|---|

ISBN: 9780170416924

# Spacing

Copy the text, then check your word spacing. Colour a small red square between each word.

The Giant Short-faced Kangaroo lived in

Australia over 15000 years ago. It is now

extinct. You can see its fossilised remains

in the Naracoorte Caves in South Australia.

*Even spacing helps to keep your handwriting legible, or easy to read.*

Rewrite each line of text with even spacing between letters and words.

The Gian t Shor t-fac ed Kang aroo was two

to thr ee metr es tall and w eig hed mor e

tha n 200 kilograms. It had a s in g le

lar g e to e on each foot an d a flat fac e.

ISBN: 9780170416924

## Self-assessment: Spacing

Practise writing with even spacing. Rewrite the text below in cursive.

The Victoria Fossil Cave is one of the

Naracoorte Caves. It hides many fossils of

ancient animals that once roamed the area.

Copy the text. Remember to maintain even spacing.

In 1969, two explorers stumbled across a

narrow gap in Victoria Fossil Cave. Inside

was a huge chamber of ancient fossils.

### Self-assessment

Rate the spacing in your handwriting.

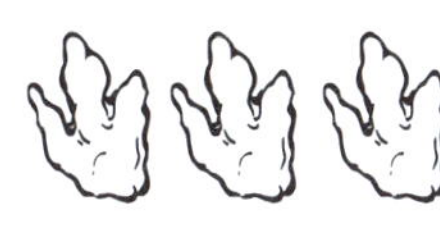

☐ It's sometimes even.

☐ It's mostly even.

☐ My spacing is always even!

ISBN: 9780170416924

# Slope

Slope lines can be drawn on the vertical parts of a letter. Using a ruler, continue to mark the slope lines in 'megafauna'.

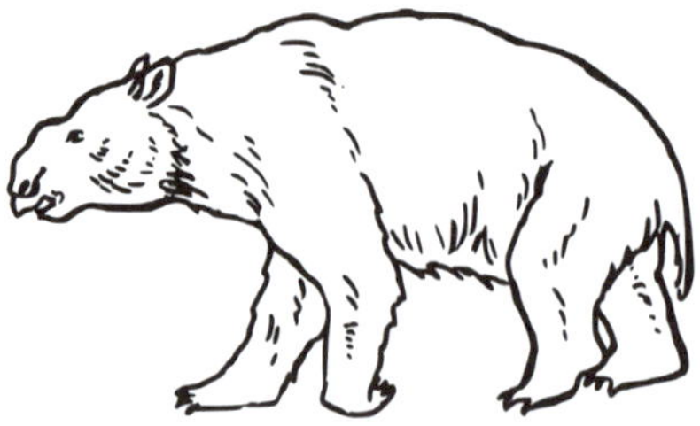

Now, write the word 'Naracoorte Caves' in cursive, using the slope lines as a guide.

Trace and finish these patterns. Try to keep a consistent slope.

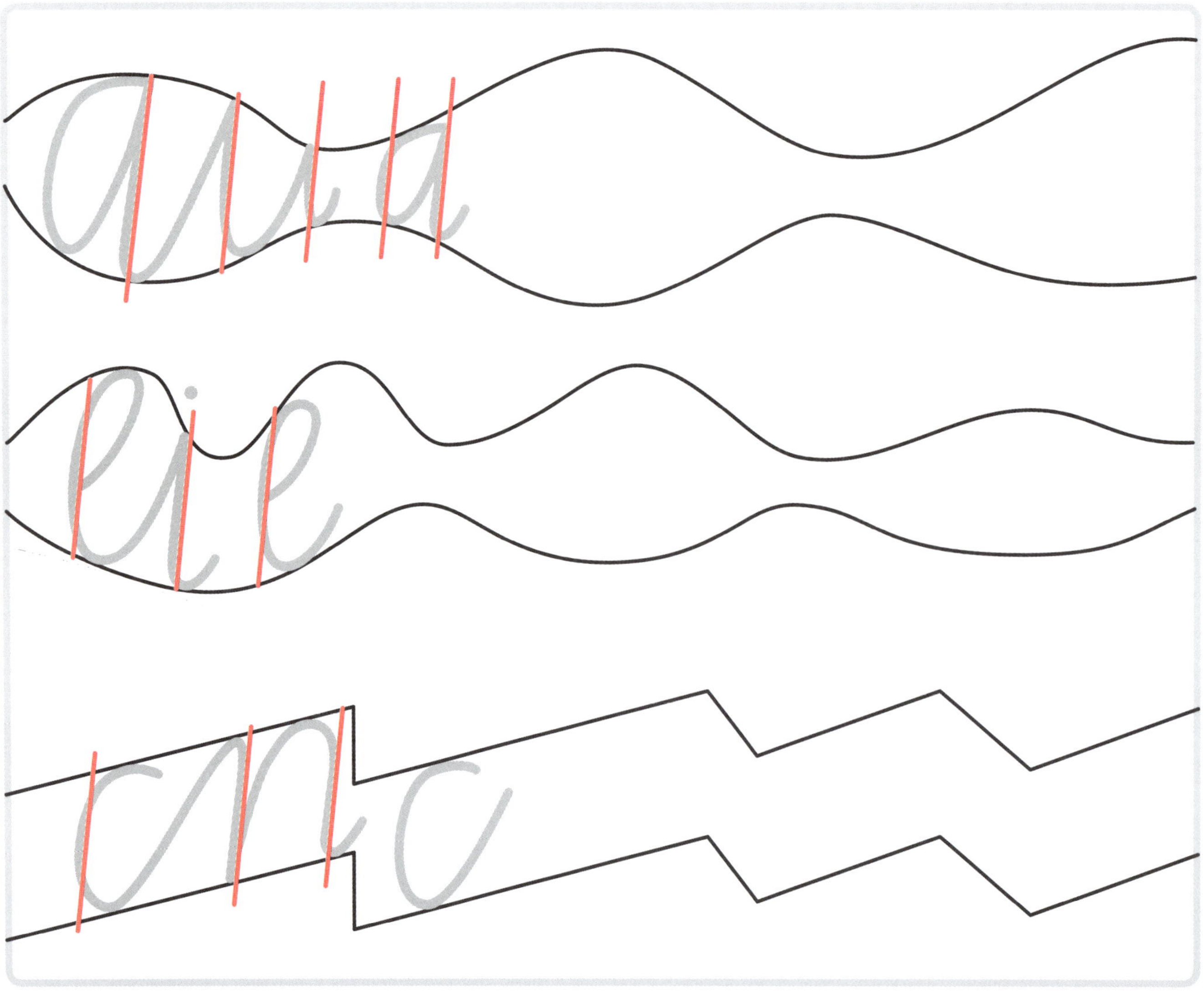

ISBN: 9780170416924

## Self-assessment: Slope

Copy these words, then check your slope. Draw slope lines on the vertical parts of the letters.

imprints ______________________

species ______________________

giant ______________________

chamber ______________________

bones ______________________

discover ______________________

get.ga/PMWA94

### Self-assessment

Rate the slope of your handwriting.

☐ I need practice.

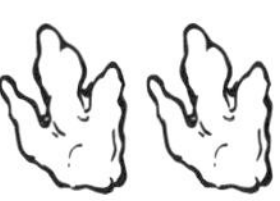

☐ My slope is sometimes consistent.

☐ My slope is always consistent!

ISBN: 9780170416924

# Joining to 's'

retrace

rs

Use a horizontal join to join top–finishing letters to the letter 's'. Make a careful horizontal sweep, then retrace the top part of 's' before completing the letter.

Kosciuszko National Park

When joining to 's' from 'f', use a straight horizontal line.

fs

Trace and copy.

os rs ws xs fs os rs ws xs fs

Kosciuszko snows cars roofs paws post

retrace

es

Use a diagonal join to join other letters to 's'. Remember to retrace.

Trace and copy.

as cs ds es is ks ls ms ns ts hs

rocks trails skis sleds ascent plains majestic

ISBN: 9780170416924

Copy the text. Remember when to use a horizontal join and when to use a diagonal join when joining to 's'.

Tessa and Lawson felt excited that 4M was having an excursion to Kosciuszko National Park. Their school bus travelled carefully up the ascent. Tessa dreamed about rushing through the snow on skis or a sled, as she looked out at the road ahead. Lawson spotted a majestic waterfall just beyond some rocky trails.

Work with a partner to order these mountain peaks from smallest to largest in elevation. Using cursive, write the mountain peaks in height order below. It might be helpful to cross off each peak as you order it correctly. Be careful when joining to the letter 's'.

Mount Twynam 2195m
Carruthers Peak 2145m
Alice Rawson Peak 2160m
Muellers Peak 2120m
Mount Kosciuszko 2228m
Mount Northcote 2131m
Mount Townsend 2209m
Rams Head 2190m

## Peer review

Ask your partner to give you some feedback on how well you wrote the text above. Ask them to notice how carefully you completed your horizontal and diagonal joins to the letter 's'.

**2 stars** (two things you did well)

**I wish** (a way for you to improve)

# Horizontal joins to 'e'

The top-finishing letters o, r, v, w and x can now join to 'e'. Use a slightly bigger dip than other horizontal joins.

bigger dip

oe re ve we xe

Trace and copy.

oe re ve we xe oe re ve we xe

Thredbo resort exercise weather

wellbeing Yarrangobilly Caves axe

creature Snowy River Alpine Way Drive

flowers rein awesome boxes area

Copy the passage below.

Thredbo is a wonderful place to stay in a ski resort and benefit from exercising in beautiful crisp mountain air. Such wonderful weather is terrific for your health and wellbeing.

The Alpine Way Drive has spectacular scenery and you may even spot a wild brumby.

These majestic horses have lived in the Mount Kosciuszko area for over 200 years.

Rewrite the passage in the box below in cursive. Take special care with your horizontal joins to 'e'.

A. B. 'Banjo' Paterson's iconic poem 'The Man from Snowy River' describes wild brumbies that run free on the mountain slopes. The poem was written in 1890 and is still read today.

## Peer review

Ask your partner to give you some feedback on how well you wrote the text above. Ask them to notice how carefully you completed your horizontal joins to the letter 'e'.

**2 stars** (two things you did well)

**I wish** (a way for you to improve)

ISBN: 9780170416924

# Joining 'ft'

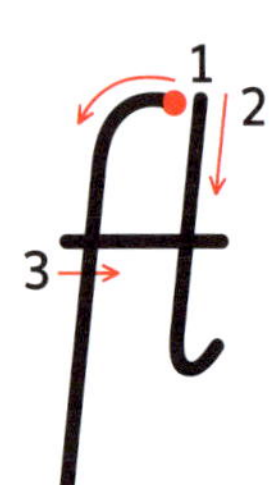

When 'f' and 't' are joined, the letters share a crossbar. Add the crossbar last of all.

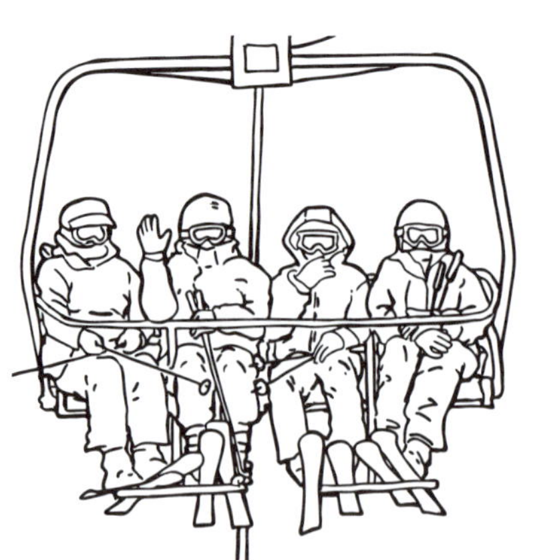

Trace and copy.

ft ft ft ft ft ft ft ft ft ft

lift swiftly soft left craft gift

tuft softly fifth loft sift twelfth

shift raft fifty draft shaft drift

Trace and copy, taking special care with your 'ft' letter pairs.

Ski lifts, sometimes known as chair lifts, are

used to carry skiers from the base of the

slopes to higher ground.

Copy the riddle below.

Q: On the fifth day of the September holidays, on the slopes of Kosciuszko, some mysterious objects were left just below the ski lifts. They were a carrot, a scarf, a hat and six pieces of coal. Why were they left there?

A: A child built a snowman and when the soft snow swiftly melted, those objects were all that was left.

ISBN: 9780170416924

Rewrite the text in the box in cursive, taking special care with your 'ft' letter pairs.

Riding a ski lift for the first time can be a challenge. It is important to pull down the safety bar once you are on the lift. After you reach the top, lift the safety bar and ski off as swiftly as you can.

## Peer review

Ask your partner to give you some feedback on how well you wrote the text above. Ask them to notice how carefully you completed your 'ft' letter pairs.

**2 stars** (two things you did well)

**I wish** (a way for you to improve)



ISBN: 9780170416924

# Using modified 's'

as → as

When joining diagonally to the letter 's', you can modify the shape of the 's' so there is less to retrace. This will help you to write faster!

Trace and copy.

as cs es ds hs ks ls ms ns ts us

sleds boots poles stocks helmets bus

slopes picks grasp horses reins muster

ascend measure bells tins rust ropes

Modified 's' is used for diagonal joins to 's'. When joining horizontally to 's', the letter 's' doesn't change. Always make your double 's's look the same.

oss iss

Trace and copy these words with horizontal joins to 's'.

Mount Alice Rawson snows expose horse

rows blows rose cross Kosciuszko

Practise joining to 's'. Copy the text.

Aisha and Hassan felt excited when their horses were led to them on ropes. They buckled their helmets and grasped the reins tightly. They mustered their courage as they descended the grassy mountainside. Next, they hit the snowy slopes with ski boots, skis and stocks. Aisha loved the rush of skiing, while Hassan preferred their time on the sleds. They were ready to rest by the time they returned to the bus.

Rewrite the text in the box in cursive, taking special care with your joins to 's'.

It is essential to consider safety when skiing. Some people descend the mountain slopes at high speeds and fail to consider other skiers. Everyone should carefully check all their equipment, including helmets, stocks and ski boots, before they head for the lifts.

SAFETY FIRST

## Peer review

Ask your partner to give you some feedback on how well you wrote the text above. Ask them to notice how carefully you completed your joins to 's'.

**2 stars** (two things you did well)

**I wish** (a way for you to improve)

# Self-assessment: Tricky joins

Copy the text below, paying careful attention to the letters with tricky joins.

It is especially lovely to explore the sensational Snowy Mountains region after the first soft snow falls. If you head left after Canberra, to historic Cooma, you can learn facts about the Snowy Mountains hydro-electricity Scheme, Australia's biggest construction project.

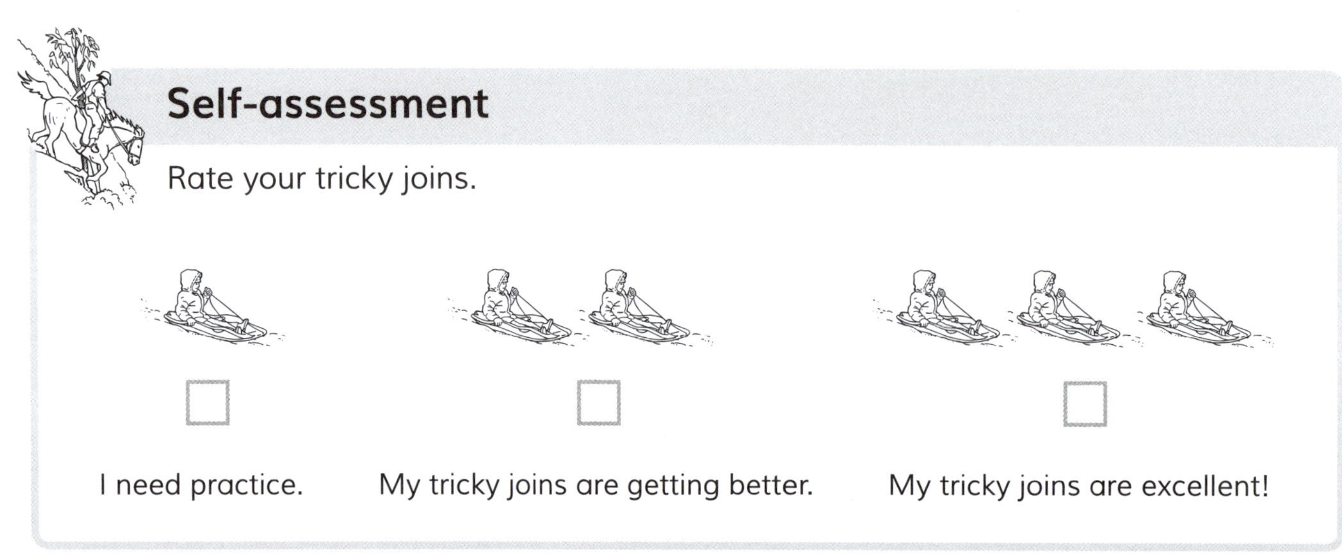

## Self-assessment

Rate your tricky joins.

- [ ] I need practice.
- [ ] My tricky joins are getting better.
- [ ] My tricky joins are excellent!

# Foundation printing

Copy the alphabet and words below.

aA bB cC dD eE fF gG hH iI

jJ kK lL mM nN oO pP qQ rR

sS tT uU vV wW xX yY zZ

Sydney volcano eroded sea shield basalt

Lord Howe Island special place forests cliffs

sandy beaches rocks undersea plateau

Rewrite the text below in Foundation printing.

Lord Howe Island is a special place. It belongs to an island group located 700 kilometres north-east of Sydney. It originated as a large shield volcano. Over time, 90% of the volcano has been eroded by the sea.

You are about to have a wonderful day on Lord Howe Island, exploring the walking tracks up the mountains and relaxing on the beautiful beaches.

Write an A–Z list of things you think you may see on your day out. Write in Foundation printing and try to think of one or two items for every letter of the alphabet.

| a<br>anemone | b<br>binoculars | c<br>catamaran |
|---|---|---|
| d | e | f |
| g | h | i |
| j | k | l |
| m | n | o |
| p | q | r |
| s | t | u |
| v | w | xyz |

ISBN: 9780170416924

# Double letter pairs

Trace and copy these double letter pairs.

bb cc dd ee gg ll

mm nn oo pp rr ss tt

Trace and copy these words with double letters.

harmless tonnes allow feeders bubbles small

supporter stunned common attractive pool

goggles seaweed craggy burrow eggs scooped

flightless rudder shallow ripple swimming

You can speed up double 'f' by using one crossbar.

1 2 3

Trace and copy.

ff different suffer off offend diffs

Copy the passage below, paying careful attention to double letter pairs.

A small, harmless insect was discovered on
Balls Pyramid, a tall, craggy outcrop off the
coast of Lord Howe Island. It is a flightless
phasmid that nearly became extinct when rats
were introduced to the island. In 2001, David
Priddel and Nicholas Carlile were stunned to
discover that there were a few of these 'land
lobster' creatures remaining. They scooped up
some eggs and Melbourne Zoo now supports a
breeding program for the rediscovered insect.

# Common letter clusters

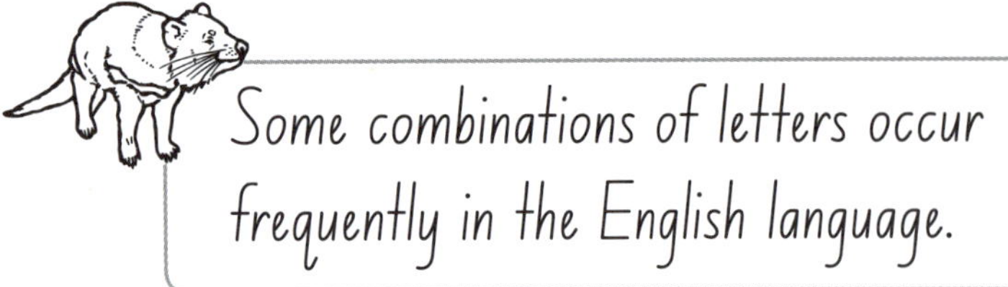

Trace and copy these common letter clusters. Copy the words.

**two-letter initial consonant blends**

bl blisters br bright cl clownfish cr crest

dr drive fl flathead fr frozen gl glisten

pr prickle sc scuba sk skip sm small

**two-letter final consonant blends**

ft lift ld fold lk walk lt halt

mp ramp nd sand ng rang nt tent

nk ink py happy rd word sk ask st best

three-letter initial consonant blends

scr scream shr shrink spl splinter

spr sprinkle squ squeal str strap thr throw

digraphs

ar car ee reel er water or fork

ch chalk ee queen sh ship th throw

ll small aw paw ay play oa boat

ou shout ow owl

Cradle Mountain

# Classifying joins

Copy the text. Then find letter pairs in the text for each join below.

The Tasmanian Wilderness is one of the last genuine wilderness regions in the world. Many people go hiking in the national parks there. One of the most photographed landmarks is Cradle Mountain, part of the Overland Trail.

diagonal joins an

drop-in joins na

horizontal joins on

joins to modified 's' ks

initial clockwise finisher ge

joins to head and body letters id

## Pencil lifts

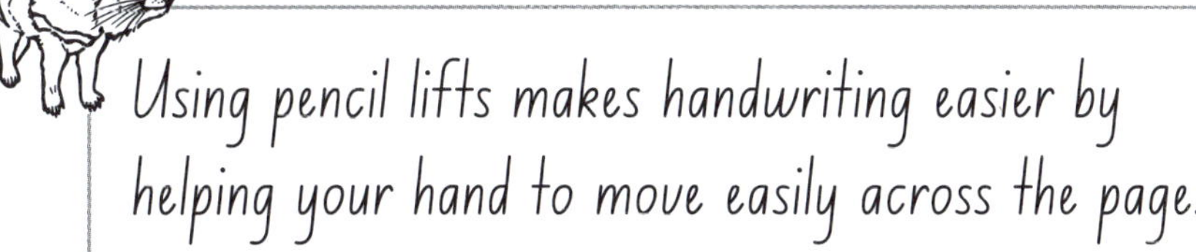

Add a dot to indicate the pencil lifts in each word. Don't forget drop-in joins.

weather eucalyptus kangaroos

bushwalking snow changeable

holiday wilderness adventure

Tasmania icicle explore vehicle

Prove your answers by writing the words above in two colours, changing colour every time you lift your pencil between letters.

# Revising drop-in joins

Remember: if you retrace the top of the anti-clockwise letters a, c, d, g and q, it slows down your handwriting. Drop-in joins are quicker.

Copy the text. Place a tick above each drop-in join.

The walking trails in Tasmania pass through

rugged, mountainous areas and unique scenery.

Make letter pairs with drop-in joins. Then use each letter pair in a word.

a c e i l u n m   to   a c d g q o f

get.ga/PMWA96

## Converting between scripts

Complete the table.

| Printing | Cursive | Capital letters |
|---|---|---|
| Tasmania | Tasmania | TASMANIA |
| | park | |
| | | PLATYPUS |
| mountain | | |
| | bushwalk | |
| | | LAKE |
| island | | |
| | beauty | |
| | | WATERFALL |
| weather | | |
| | tourists | |
| | | FLORA |
| fauna | | |
| | wombat | |
| | | SPECIES |

Circle the script you find most comfortable to write.

printing cursive CAPITALS

# Numerals

Read the facts, then copy the numerals and number words below.

- The Tasmanian Wilderness is $\frac{1}{5}$ of the area of the state.
- The Overland Track is 73 km long.
- Tasmania is 240 km south of the Australian mainland.
- Tasmania is the 26th largest island in the world.
- An adult male Tasmanian devil is about 65 cm in length, and weighs up to 12 kg.

$\frac{1}{5}$ one-fifth

73 km seventy-three kilometres

240 km two hundred and forty kilometres

26th twenty-sixth

65 cm sixty-five centimetres

12 kg twelve kilograms

# Revising size, spacing and slope

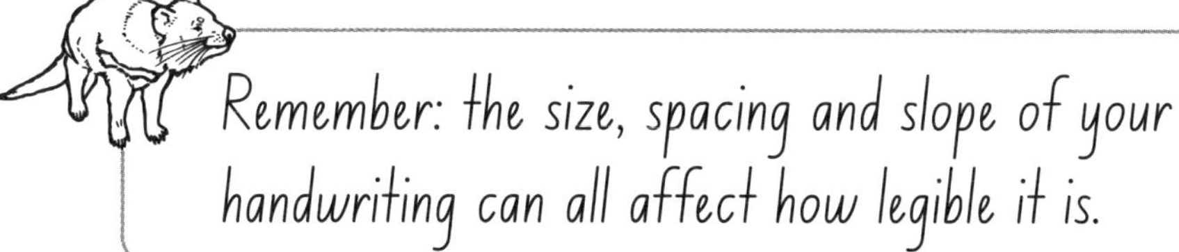


Copy these words in the spaces provided. Be careful to keep the size of your letters the same as the models.

geography Tasmania hiking mapping

distance mountain fieldwork track

climb adventure cold protect bushland

environment country kinship respect

Sometimes you need to write at a different size. Can you change the size of your writing and maintain your legibility?

walk walk walk walk

Rewrite the text in the box in cursive, then check your word spacing. Colour a small red square between each word.

Tasmanian devils can be found in the wild in Tasmania. Devils became extinct on the mainland thousands of years ago. They are now endangered in Tasmania, too.

Rewrite the text below with correct letter spacing.

A Tasmania n tiger was the size of a dog.

It had st ripe s on its back an d a

pouc h lik e a kan gar oo.

Copy the text, then check your slope. Draw slope lines on the vertical parts of the letters.

Tasmanian devils are black but can have

white fur on their rump or chest.

Practise writing the word 'legible' three times, using the slope lines as a guide.

legible

Now write a word of your own.

Trace and copy these patterns. Try to maintain an even slope.

fff lll elele

# Building endurance in handwriting

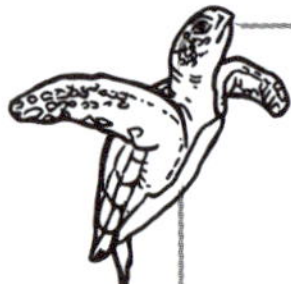

Regular handwriting practice helps to build endurance: the ability to write a lot of text at the one time.

Rewrite the text in the box below in your best cursive handwriting.

My visit to the reef was fascinating! As soon as I put my mask on the surface of the water, I had an incredible view of this marine environment. The purple and pink colours of the coral were quite striking.
I saw a school of several clownfish swimming along together.

# Joins revision

Test your knowledge of joins. Copy the words, then identify the letter pairs using the join in each group.

**drop-in join pairs**

magnificent unhappy amazement

ma

**diagonal join pairs**

dangerous hundred afterwards

**horizontal join pairs**

crouch underground strongest

**clockwise finishing letters**

properly smoothly join straight

get.ga/PMWA97

## Final self-assessment

Copy the text.

The Whale Shark is the largest fish in the sea. It is as large as many whales but it is a fish, not a mammal. The mouth of a Whale Shark can be up to 1.5 metres wide and can contain 300 rows of tiny teeth. Even though the Whale Shark is a fish, it is a filter feeder like many whales.

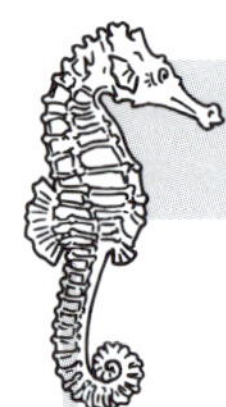

### Self-assessment

Rate the legibility of your NSW Foundation style cursive.

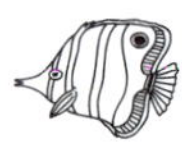

☐ It's getting there.

☐ It's good.

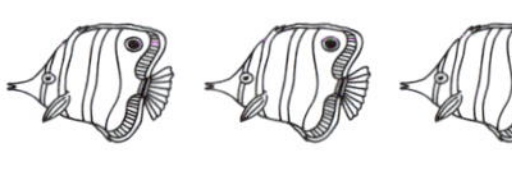

☐ My cursive is excellent!

# Mapping a journey around Australia

Label the states and territories of Australia on the map. Use capital letters.

Draw the Aboriginal flag below and use the correct colours to colour it in.

# Teacher observation guide

Student is: left-handed ☐ right-handed ☐

Student demonstrates correct posture, paper position and pencil grip. ☐

Student uses writing lines with accuracy. ☐

Student forms NSW Foundation style printing (lower-case and capital letters) with accuracy. ☐

Student can write numerals with accuracy. ☐

Student forms the exit and entry letters with accuracy, including the modified 'f'. ☐

Student forms the following joins with accuracy:

- diagonal joins ☐
- drop-in joins ☐
- horizontal joins ☐
- diagonal joins from 'q' ☐
- diagonal joins from 'z' ☐
- horizontal joins from 'f' ☐
- joins to 's' ☐
- horizontal joins to 'e' ☐
- 'ft' joins ☐

Student can identify the letters that do not join in NSW Foundation style cursive. ☐

Student can convert between scripts: printing, cursive and capital letters. ☐

Student can copy a complete passage of text with accuracy using NSW Foundation style cursive. ☐

Student can identify when a pencil lift is required. ☐

Student has an understanding of factors that influence legibility (size, spacing, slope). ☐

Student can self-assess with accuracy. ☐

*Notes:*

..................................................................................................................

..................................................................................................................

Date:

......................................................................

CERTIFICATE

get.ga/PMWC90